The Understanding Repentance

Sophia Calloway

Copyright © 2012 Sophia Calloway

All rights reserved.

ISBN: **0615641628**
ISBN-13: **978-0615641621**

DEDICATION

This book is dedicated to
The Father, His Son and His Holy Spirit

CONTENTS

	Acknowledgments	i
1	Understanding our Heritage	17
2	Adam and God's Church	Pg 27
3	The Figment Tree	Pg 33
4	Sight and Separation	Pg 37
5	The Responses	Pg 42
6	Satan's Motives	Pg 45
7	The Tree of Life	Pg 48
8	Sin, Love and Honor	Pg 54
9	Understanding 666	Pg 62
10	God's Accounting Methods	Pg 89
11	Crowning Conclusion	Pg 90
12	The Ten Commandment	Pg 108

ACKNOWLEDGMENTS

I acknowledge the Power of the Father
in the relaying of this book to you.
I pray the veil begin to be lifted
and you will come to Christ and that
your veil be lifted out of
His love and care for you.
To Him be all the glory.

i

THIS BOOK IS INTENTIONALLY WRITTEN SO THAT YOU WILL STUDY AND FIND SCRIPTURES ON YOUR OWN, PRAY FOR THE HOLY SPIRIT TO TEACH YOU AS YOU READ

CHAPTER ONE UNDERSTANDING

OUR HERITAGE

It IS WRITTEN that God so loved the world, that He gave His only (begotten Son) that whosoever (whomever chooses) believes in Him (understands, trusts and relies in His Person and Authority with confidence), shall have Eternal Life. (The intimate understanding and knowledge of the Father).

The Father so much loved us, that He gave us His only Son. It's almost difficult to understand how much God loves us. He knew us before we were born. We were thought and spoken out of the generational and spiritual womb of God. We were in Him and resided in His thoughts and were ever present in His glory. When it was time for us to be formed, He began with the first soul and His name was Adam. Adam (the name) when translated, holds the definition of Man. Man was not born, for he was formed from the very thoughts of our heavenly Father. Adam was a replica of what was in heaven. A piece of heaven was formed from the ground and Adam became a living soul, after the Spirit of God caused and allowed him to breathe. With the breath of God in His lungs and nostrils, Adam literally breathed through the breath of His Father. This is the same as you and I today. Every breath you take is from God's own mouth and without it naturally flowing through you, it is impossible for you to live. Our Father gave us a new lineage that was to serve Him on the earth. This was a new era in the realms or territories of our Father's ruler ship in the universe.

This was the beginning of a new generation. It is as it is now again, a new era in the heavens and earth. It is the righteous ruling by the Governmental Authority and Order of our Father the King.

When our Father created the universe, His Spirit which is His Power, His Will and the Essence of All, perpetuated or caused all He spoke, to come alive before Him according the Will of the Father. Therefore the Spirit of God, does the Will of God, not in Words, for the Word has already been spoken, but by Power

It's not our desire or our will that our Father demonstrates His power to perform; for we do not have that authority. However when we are in Him and He is in us, it is He that commands His will to be done in our lives.. It is then that, that Will or Order is brought forth by His own Power and Spirit.

By the Word and Will of our Father and for His own purposes, He created mankind to perform the works necessary to rule in His Kingdom. We cannot do these works or instructions without His authority or command. Therefore without His permission, we can do nothing.

Adam (man) was created to do the will of our Father, as we are created to do the Will of our Father as well. We cannot do His Will if we are disobedient to it, if we don't take responsibility for it, or deny or misuse it. The fact is this; our Father's will is His desire, not the reverse.

When our desires come in alignment with His desires, we are made fit to serve in His Kingdom, and to do on earth as it is in heaven. Therefore whatever we do that is alignment with our Father in heaven is in alignment with our Father as we do it upon the earth. Agreement with Him is paramount, but we first must be open to His Truth and be willing to be taught His Ways.

Many can talk about Him; many can speak of all the promises and wonderful things He has accomplished in their own personal as well as other people's lives. However do not have the relationship necessary to bring you into the Power and Presence of God the Almighty. False religion and its benefactors do not hold that type of Power. To walk in His Power and Authority, one has to have an understanding of how He wishes for you comprehend what the Godhead is all about.

In order to understand our Father, He gave us His Son. In order to understand Jesus, we must understand the Father. In order to understand the relationship between the two of them, we must know the Father first; and then we must look to the Son.

All things are to be done decently and in order. Without His order and without revelation, there can be no Truth Church, for the church is built on the revelation of knowing of the Godhead as they have always and ever will be. This is the premise and the foundation of the True Church; the Bride of Christ.

We build on a foundation and the foundation is written and revealed by the Father and given to Jesus to perform and brought into manifestation by His Spirit which is His power.

False interpretations of how to build that foundation remain the basis of any fall. Our Father builds on His interpretation of His Word and not ours. He is the one that decides what is to be built, how it is to be built and when it is to be completed. He decides who is to partake of it, how it is to be run and who has His Authority to use His Name. Those who do not use His Name appropriately and with permission or commission, use His Name in vain.

These are those who have stolen the True Identity of Christ.

Those who practice this behavior are in the total violation of the instructions of God as they are written in His commandments or "commands meant for men."

Religion has taught us to be obedient out of precepts of strict conditions. These involve a misuse or manipulation of scripture resulting in private interpretation, thus bringing forth false promises of Christ.

Instead of serving God because of what He does for us, most will serve God thinking that they will receive materialistic riches, while others are taught to serve out of fear. These individuals end up believing that God is going to do something evil to them, even though they are if they fall or make a mistake.

Most have been taught that we must sacrifice ourselves, by putting ourselves through pain and agony in order to please Him. Yet still others believe they have to make amends with God, by giving money, while leaving the ones that have been wronged desolate. Religion has brought more fear on people because it has taught people to fear God and have used the word "fear" out of context.

The word fear is to be used as a "reverence" term. It is not to be used to instill anxiety in people. We have seen the many cases in the bible where people have been struck down, but it wasn't because God retaliating because He hated them. That would be nonsense. However Our Father does respond in a particular manner, because of their disobedience to His instructions. Thus lending themselves to evil, thus provokes God's hand to anger.

Do not believe people who say to you that God is going to get you if you don't give or if you don't do what they tell you to do. There are too many false prophets in the world trying to get your money in the hopes of promoting themselves and not God. Beware of these people. God will always validate His Word **With** Power A lot of people will give you "a word" but few back it up with the almighty Power of God.

Our Father has built in boundaries and protections to keep us from evil, if we choose to believe in Him.

CHAPTER TWO

ADAM AND GOD'S CHURCH

When He created Adam (man), we can see the great deal of protectiveness He had in mind when His Spirit hovered over the place where He wanted His heavenly offspring to rule and reside.

At the beginning of this world, everything was created so that man could enjoy a relationship with their Father, while enjoying a paradise. The world was filled with beautiful skies, rivers of waters and a garden filled with everything that man could ever want. Mankind had no need for anything else; after all; He is our Father and our Father is the Great Provider.

Adam (man) had everything and upon our Father placing him there, he was given instructions to live in this vast garden. Our Father placed him east of Eden and he was assigned to rule and to tend to that portion of it.

Eden symbolically represents God's church. Man was placed in it to tend to it and to keep it. He questioned Adam to see if he could name the animals' names. His spirit, motives and intellect were tested. Upon passing, God gave him everything. Adam showed He could intellectually rule in His Church.

The next thing He did was form Eve. Eve was formed from Adam's rib. Rib when translated means "side." Thus, Eve came out of Adam side while he was asleep.

Eve represents the church that comes out of man. Eve was not formed until Adam could pass the test of recounting the animal's names.

An animal represents our lower or carnal selves. Therefore we can understand that we must see God's kingdom and beasts as they are, as well as call identify them as they are. Until then we are not fit yet to rule in the positions of His Authority that all intimately seek to desire.

The Father tested him intimately. This means He tested the inmost thoughts and desires of his heart. He tested his character to see if he would follow instructions. He tested him as an individual, and then gave him his wife.

In biblical terms the wife is the bride and bride is the bride of Christ which is the church. The church is the

Word of God. Therefore Adam was given the church to be by his side. He was to watch over it and protect it as He did with the garden. He was to love her as He loves His own wife.

Adam and Eve were the first representatives of what our Father meant for us to have on this earth. They were the blueprint for mankind, so that people could see the invisible God. The bible states that Adam became a "living soul." The soul represents the inner person or the inner man. Thus our Father created His inner being. Out of that inner man came Eve. Eve was born out of that inner man which is the church. The church is pure Word of God and the Word of God is Christ and Christ is the Son of God, who is in Our Father.

This complete circle was a ring that unites all in one perfect union. Our Father was in them, they were in the Father. It was total agreement between them all. It was a marriage, a vow of bonds between the Father and Mankind. When there is unity, no one sees where the bond ring begins or ends. These are the binding vows of eternal life. They are intertwined and are seen in this manner.

The first ring was how the garden or church responded to Christ. All things, all creatures and all trees in the garden responded to His voice and did accordingly. They did not respond because they had to, but they responded because of the reverence given to Whom had created them.

The second ring was given to man to respond just as the all that lived in the garden responded.

To understand this we look to the parable of the mustard seed.

The Word says that if we have faith as a mustard seed, we would be able to speak to a mountain and it would move. What religion has not taught is that the mustard seed responded to the Father's voice and reacted. In other words the mustard seed itself had faith. The mustard seed had the faith of Jesus in it, because Jesus Himself obeyed as a mustard seed.

We cannot have the faith of God if we do not have faith in God. He is Alpha and Omega. He is the Beginning and the End.

It is our reasonable service to adhere to His instructions. If it were not for Him we would not have the ability to live. Without His permission and authority we cannot function properly, for without Him there is no existence.

When our Father created man and the church, He was happy with them. He walked with what He had made; being the inner man and His church. However as we know this union was not to last in the manner that it was created.

Man fell into a state of selfishness and complacency. He did not watch over what was given to him to tend. He had everything he desired. He had a wife, a garden and a paradise to enjoy his work. This left an opening for deceit and self reliance to kick in.

When Adam was given his instructions, the Father visited and walked with him on a daily basis. This shows us that Adam was left on His own to tend over what God had given Him. He was given the extra responsibility now to tend over his wife, (the church).

When we read the Word it states that out of man's mouth concerning Eve (the church), "flesh of my flesh and bone of my bone."

We know that Eve wandered, but she could not have wandered if this was not already in Adam's (man's) mind. Why? It is because Eve was taken "**out** of man."

We are to look at Man as in the Generation of Mankind.

Therefore this side of Adam (man) was taken out and shown to him. It was man's job to look at it and tend to it. In other words Adam was to tend to what God was showing Him concerning His church, just as he would in regards to his wife and bride.

Consequently Adam refused to look at it or her for what she was doing. In other words He did not want to look at what He didn't want to see.

When the serpent spoke to man's flesh, man's flesh responded to the serpent, but that same flesh didn't respond to the Father. Therefore they gave ear to hear a serpent and not to our Father.

The bible says Eve saw that the Tree of the Knowledge of Good and Evil was good for food and had the ability to make one wise. Jesus is known as the Bread of Life or Truth Doctrine. This tree was good for food. Since they were not to touch it; it is determined that it is food that is not pure or for mortal consumption.

Man and his wife, (the church) were already warned not to eat of that tree. (To eat of the tree is to ingest its fruit and to savor its flavor). They had already been given the boundaries of protection and Adam already proved himself to be a good steward with obedience to the Father. Man's capabilities and faculties were tested first and now it was time to test his character. For this reason he would have no excuse that he didn't understand what our Father was teaching him to do. It was time to test the inner man in regards to His church. It was time to test and show mankind that man cannot do things alone.

Now keep in mind that Eve had the characteristics of Adam already. They were of one mind and one body. Though they were separate they were one in thought, mind and deed. She was taken out of him. But as stated earlier; what man doesn't want to look at and refuses to see in time will eventually die.

The serpent knowing this, knew exactly what they wanted to hear. When the story of Adam and Eve is told, Eve is made out to be the cause of the falling out. But it was Adam's responsibility, because without him there would be no Eve. What was in Adam was part of Eve. Hence this is why Adam accompanied her to the Tree of Knowledge of Good and Evil. He too was lured into what was already on his mind. He was also being shown what was in him that was fleshy, carnal and animalistic. He was to tend and rule over those things.

When they wandered, Eve saw that the tree was desirable for food and had the ability to make one wise. This was a tree that had the characteristics of good and evil and it is compared to a fig tree or tree of unripe fruit.

It is a tree that bears the combination of holy and unholy doctrine. The serpent was around it, because he is wrapped up in it. He has mixed himself in it. He has twisted the doctrine just as he is twisted as a serpent. It is the doctrine of polluted or dirty truth.

The words "fig tree" literally mean in Hebrew, unripe fruit. The characteristics of this doctrine involve our Father, but also involve buying and selling twisted doctrine and saying that it is the Father's will and purpose; or the Father's will and testament.

The word "doctrine "literally means "What is received as truth."

These doctrines entertain those who are buying and selling our Father's peace in the form of false prophecies.

A prophecy is God's Word which is accompanied by a promise. This promise is fulfilled by God's vow to you. Thus, He swears with His right Hand, that He will do His Word. Since it is impossible for Him to lie and void the Truth, every prophecy or promise in scripture, must come to pass. Therefore our Father warns people not to privately interpret something he never said. This will only result in rebellion and will make Him appear as a liar. These false prophecies or explanations of doctrine are given by those who hide lies within the Truth.

These are those who hold false offices in manmade buildings and those who have appointed themselves; thus establishing their rebellion against our Father.

These are those who are buying and selling goods and services and doing business in and through the church. These are those who use the word of God as shortcuts to getting rich or prospering in a material or worldly manner. These are those who turn the Word of God into a center for spiritual trafficking. Just like human trafficking, they sell out their congregants with sermons which involve sowing to get money and "get rich schemes" they claim are established by God Himself

These are those who are entertaining the barter system within the church for business hookups and the interaction between individuals to find mates or girl/boyfriends and/or husbands. These are those who trade the freedom of proclaiming the gospel in order to barter for a tax deduction.

These are those who buy and sell their goods such as their God given talents, in order to make money from those attending in these congregations. They perform and disguise it as worship, when it is really entertainment to propel them into the worldly level. It is validated through the advertisement following their performance of where you can purchase their books or CDs.

These are those who buy and sell, thus turning the church into a business rather than a House of Prayer.

This tree is for the buying and selling of merchandise and the enforcement of twisted doctrine. These doctrines mesmerize man, just as they did to Adam and Eve.

Those practicing these doctrines are those who carved images made of different materials and they put His Name upon them. These are those who call their leader" father" or" holy" when the Bible states no man is holy and we are to call no man father except him that is in heaven.

These are those who claim themselves in identity as a god, by simply denying His True message and testimony.

These are those who dressed in royal robes and extravagant suits, in order to show how holy and blessed they are.

These are those who profess that man can take away or has the recipe to take away your sins. These are the ones who promote themselves with grand titles and positions, in order to convince you that they are the Chosen of God.

These are those who would rather serve each other, rather than serving Him.

These are those who provide prayer recipes for their sin and that sin.

These are those who believe" the riches of his glory" are the material wealth God has given. These are those who advertise their conferences and seminars over and over and charging admission for you to gain the Truth.

These are those who sell tickets to their holy assemblies, while having those who cannot afford out in the cold.

These are those who have turned the Holy Spirit into a" babbling disgrace, performing false miracles through the use of self imaginations and or demons.

These are those who buy and sell their ideas dressed up as God. Their imaginations lure you in and your inner man thus making you accountable as well as indebted to them and the power they serve.

These are the things that Satan uses for your food. In other words, what they have is good to look at and it fueled by your emotions and feelings. This doctrine lures the inner man and the church at the same time. But it cannot lure the church without the tempting the inner man first.

CHAPTER THREE

BREAKING DOWN OF FOOD

This tree fig tree was not ripe. In order for fruit to ripen it has to go through a ripening process. Many things happen as fruit ripens.

Unripe fruit is often green, sour, odorless, hard and mealy. The ripening process makes the fruit more appealing. The color of the skin changes as chlorophyll (the green stuff in plants) is broken down and in some cases new pigments are made.

The acids that make the fruit sour are broken down, then the mealy starches are converted into sugar and then hard pectin is softened. Larger molecules are made into smaller ones that then cause them to evaporate as aroma. Suddenly, we have a soft, juicy, sweet, fragrant, colorful animal-attractor.

If we parallel this with God's word we see preachers of all kinds giving the Word of God in the same manner.

Instead of giving it to you whole so that you can enjoy the fullness of it, they are converting or translating it so that it is easy to eat.

This is done by breaking down a verse here and a verse there and combining it, so that it is desirable for you to eat. The verses are broken down to an interpretation and made into an idea rather than the Truth. This doctrine therefore is spoken through your thoughts, which later are converted to prayers. They are the sour aroma that believes that God the Almighty is pleased to accept. They have created a god and it is to that god that they speak to. It is a god with no breath and no life; for it is just a "figment" of something that is not real.

These ideas are fed to the people in both the people causing their leaders get fat from the lies. Then they are led to believe that God will show up and do it all for them. Consequently they inadvertently and subsequently make themselves into gods.

Each idea or molecule rouses the imaginations and excites the senses. These ideas are strengthened through the use of talents and riches of the leaders who partake of it.

They lure you into their man made buildings. Great statues of holiness and works of art that cause you to look at images of what they believe our Father and biblical characters look like.

They tempt you with the riches of their material wealth, with the buildings they have constructed to hold thousands of people.

Their charisma or charm is equivalent to that of snake charmer, but just as a snake charmer fascinates you with his power over serpents; these individuals have no snake, they just make you believe that one is alive to bite you at every turn.

Their attire has the appeal to tempt your senses and rouse you to start to believe what holiness is supposed to look like. This twisted doctrine fascinates the hearer and the seer with what appears to be sweet, fragrant and juicy. But most of all, it appeals to the carnal, animalistic tendencies of man.

Those who have ingested this doctrine use the Scriptures as recipes and have turned holy verses into incantations.

Their prayers are written in books for the entire world to see and are used as directions to get this or get that.

These are those who take verses out of context and twist them in order to provide fascination and to make it and the person giving it more attractive and seemingly more powerful.

When the people believe they are powerful, they believe their leader is powerful. Thus from this belief they establish that they can make fruit on their own; only this fruit is from the combination of good and evil. This is what I have called mankind giving the bible "a produce makeover."

This "produce makeover" has parallels in fruit as well as in people. This makeover is unique as it requires a group of enzymes in plants to react on cue.

In the human condition, those attending conferences or churches, are taught subliminally and react and act on cue, in response to the tempo and style of music and the tone and volume of which a leader speaks. It is a manner of hypnotism disguised as God's Spirit or their version of the Holy Spirit.

Some will tell you that God lives in their building while others will say God shows up in the atmosphere or in the air. Air itself is a type of gas that is in our atmosphere. Sin produces its own air and perpetuates the "airs" that people tend to put on given to the religious vehicles they travel within.

Gas does not have an independent shape or quality, but it does have the capability to expand indefinitely. Therefore because of this ability there is no end to what they can do, unless our Father steps into the picture.

These individuals feel through their emotions and equate their experiences as the manifestation of God's glory. These "moments" are fuelled by self appreciation, to make one think they are so powerful that they can change the atmosphere, (hence the air description).

Since this gas is in the air, all things spoken are in and from the air. Satan is commanded by God to rule the air, so it is he of whom these speak. These include talking in baby language or vowel sounds.

These preachers are subtle in their teaching and the verses are so broken down that they are misunderstood. In the end the scriptures have lost not only their meaning, but also the power behind what they were intended to bring forth.. Therefore it is easy to manipulate and signal the group, once certain manifestations are to take place.

In plants they take their cue from a ripening signal, which in actuality is a burst of gas called ethylene. Ethylene is a simple hydrocarbon gas produced when a fruit ripens. Ethylene flips the switch to trigger the genes that in turn make the enzymes that cause ripening.

Therefore, just as sin is in our DNA, the gasoline that fuels the sin is there also.

Man's inner self is the seat of thought and emotions. Just as plants send signals all the time using hormones, so goes with mankind.

In plants this ripening signal is unique, because it involves an airborne hormone called Ethylene. It is produced by rapidly growing tissue (the tips of roots, flowers, ripening fruit, and damaged tissue). Thus, a wound can activate ethylene production; just the act of picking green fruit can cause the ripening process to begin.

Just as hormones cause these processes to begin so our people's emotions, as their hormones are the emotional fuel that affects their desires.

Man was told not to eat and not to touch the fruit of the Tree of the Knowledge of Good and Evil. When we eat of that tree we are not only sentenced to death, but we end up crucifying Christ over and over again, whether it be by action, word or practice.

We are "not to touch or go near" these doctrines of men. It is a direct violation against the instructions and commands of

God. He also compares this doctrine as that which is associated with winds and waves, which is blown over and away because it is not built on a solid foundation.

Jesus said that we will know them by their fruit. What type of fruit is being produced? A good and pure tree produces good fruit and a bad tree or a fig tree produces bad fruit.

CHAPTER FOUR

THE FIGMENT TREE

Now you may be asking how do we know that this was a fig tree.

In Mark Chapter Eleven, Jesus and His disciples were walking along the road and Jesus saw a fig tree. He cursed the fig tree and said "May no fruit ever again grow on you." He did this within the disciples hearing. Immediately after cursing the fig tree, He was in the temple courts driving out the money changers.

These are those who were conducting their own business instead of our Father's business. These are the ones who were and are promoting or selling different doves; for these symbolize the different versions of the Holy Spirit. He drove out everyone who did not operate God's house, as a House of Prayer.

On the way back after this event, Jesus and His disciples came upon the fig tree once again. This time it was withered to the roots.

His first response to them when they asked what had happened to them was "Have faith in God." In the next sentence He says:

"For assuredly, I say to you, whoever says to this mountain, 'Be removed and be cast into the sea,' and does not doubt in his heart, but believes that those things he says will be done, he will have whatever he says.[24] Therefore I say to you, whatever things you ask when you pray, believe that you receive *them,* and you will have *them.*[25] "And whenever you stand praying, if you have anything against anyone, forgive him, that your Father in heaven may also forgive you your trespasses. [26] But if you do not forgive, neither will your Father in heaven forgive your trespasses."

The verse says that if you do not doubt in your heart.

Religions have taught in the context that if you wish with all your heart, you are not in doubt; so if you wish with all your heart, you will receive what you ask for. Wrong!

Doubt is lack of trust that someone is not telling the truth in regards to what they have not yet seen in order to believe. Doubt deals with trust and reliance. It comes from not knowing the one you are trusting in. True trust comes from those you know, not those you don't know.

However how can one trust if they do not understand in Whom they are to trust?

When understood correctly the heart is where the eyes of understanding make their rest. The eyes of our understanding lie in our heart. Thus without understanding and comprehending the true intentions of Our Father and agreeing with them, what you ask WILL NOT be done for you by the Father.

Therefore in order not to have doubt, you must have an understanding. An understanding is a true comprehension of what cannot be seen. Without it we will not be able to comprehend He that has apprehended us.

Having said that if we do not doubt in our hearts, we can comprehend what He is actually trying to tell us. So therefore, doubt will leave when you have an understanding, because the understanding builds trust.

Therefore, if you understand the purposes of God in your heart, you will have what you ask for and whatever you ask will be done for you. This is because you will already know what He approves of and what He does not.

However with no understanding you will seek him with the wrong heart or motive, and He will not reveal Himself.

A revelation is not learned. It is given only by God. David said" create in me a new heart oh Lord." We need to do the same so that we may have personal revelation of not only Him but also His ways.

Speaking for something to be done is only half the equation. It must be followed with understanding.

We must seek comprehension within scriptural context, in order to see the fullness of the purposes of what our Father has in His mind. It is then that we can ask according to His Will. For whatever we ask according to the Will of the Father, it shall be done. Thus this validates His Word in how He instructed His disciples to pray:

Thy Kingdom come, Thy Will be done, on earth as it is in heaven.

In the case of the fig tree, the tree was cursed (cut off) because it did not bear the fruit that the Father was looking for. Just as with Adam and Eve, the fig tree was cursed because it did not provide the fruit that the Father wanted us to indulge and were not even to go near.

.

CHAPTER FIVE SIGHT AND SEPARATION

When Adam (man) and Eve (church) took their instructions from twisted doctrine, they turned and had faith in what a serpent, an animal, and a beast was telling them. In this very act, they denied our Father, who graciously had provided for them, but their fleshiness and carnality, accompanied by their animalistic tendencies, caused them to turn the other way. Their spirit, their inner man, was now polluted and tainted by a food that was not agreeable with them.

Our Father had clothed them in His glory. Their Spirit was our Father's Spirit.

They lived and breathed with the air that He had placed within their souls. He fed them with the purity of His

Word and in the understanding they were to have. Their souls (inner man) were cloaked in the purity of His Glory. They had resembled our Father in both Spirit and Truth. But now they were separated from His Glory.

They were joined in union with one another. Before the contamination, they were of One breath and One accord. God's very Presence was the essence of their being. However when they wandered and listened to another voice, that was not our Father's, they made an error and a huge mistake in judgment. Not only that but they denied their Father three times.

Thus by simply going against the instructions (law made by the Father), they fell into rebellion and therefore sin; which causes separation. One could perceive it as a type of divorce.

The bible states that the eyes of both of them were opened and they knew they were naked. The eyes of good were opened and the eyes of evil were opened simultaneously.

Some of the translated words for eyes are: appearance, forehead, eyesight, thoughts and fountain.

Therefore what was in evil now made its appearance to their eyes and to their thoughts. They opened a mixture that would cause them to be like a god. To be like a god, you do not have to "know" Him; meaning you don't have to intimately have communication and relationship with

Him. All you have to do is have the appearance that you know Him.

When these eyes were opened, they were aware through their own thoughts and intelligence that they were naked.

The Father had asked them "who told you that you were naked?" God created and clothed the spiritual inner man in the both of them. Consequently we now understand the significance of seeing themselves naked. For how could they see their inner man when our inner man cannot be seen with the naked eye?

It was because the eyes of their understanding were opened. What they could not see before now was in the open and they were put to shame. They not only shamed themselves but shamed the Father as well.

They ate of the two doctrines and became wise in their own eyes.

The bible does not say they left the tree to clothe themselves. Eve (church) and Adam (man) sewed the fig leaves together and wrapped them around their waist. Therefore they were no longer clothed in the purity of our Father, for now they were clothed by what they have sewn together their own doctrine and then dressed themselves.

Like a writer who sews a yarn or a tale, so these also clothed themselves in a story that was filled with impurities. Their Holy Spirit was now unclean. They sewed together leaves from a tree that was of no use and no good purpose. They girded these about their waist as truth.

This is in contrast to the armor of God as stated in Ephesians, where we are to be girded with the belt of Truth around our waist.

The King James Version states they made themselves aprons from fig leaves. When the word "aprons" is translated, it is defined as an armor or belt. Therefore they clothed themselves with mixed doctrine and it was not until that point that man had to answer to our Father and also for Eve (the church).

Anyone who is guilty is shown by God their shame. Guilt and shame causes one to have the tendency to run or flee for the safety of a hiding place.

When the Father called out to Adam (man), He asked Him where he was in the garden. In a sense He was asking him why he turned and regressed into a lower being.

He then asked man questions pertaining to accountability. It obviously touched the Father's presence because sin had entered into the Most Holy Place; His church. What was clothed in holiness and purity was now dressed in mixed doctrine.

Adam became the embodiment of what he received from the tree. He could not have received it, if he didn't believe it.

When God questioned both of them to hold them accountable, their answers were not honest, but shifty in nature. They admitted to no responsibility for their actions. Three times they gave excuses or reasons for their behavior, instead of acknowledging their wrong doings and coming to repentance.

Instead of holding one another accountable to each other, now they themselves were not willing to be accountable to our Father either.

CHAPTER SIX

THE RESPONSES

Their first response was non chalant. Adam (man) gave an answer that he thought God wanted to hear, while at the same time hiding himself. This was an attempt to hide the lie in the Truth, thus contaminating or concealing the Truth.

The word "hid" when translated means to draw back. Man could not have known to draw back, unless he knew he had already erred in judgment.

Our Father is holy and anything that is not holy will draw back or fall back from His Presence, for they cannot stand in the Almighty God. Therefore when man drew back and hid, it was done out of shrewdness and craftiness, in the hopes that He would not see what they had done.

There was no repentance involved. It was more of "I'll wait and see if He sees me" attitude.

The second answer was in response to accountability as well as responsibility. Adam took the responsibility placed on him and placed it on Eve. In other words, man was saying "It's the church's fault." The church gave the doctrine and therefore I'm not responsible for what I have been fed."

Since Eve (church) came out of man and the church is the reflection of man,(just as the wife is the reflection of the husband), God asked the church (Eve), what she had done. The church answered God and said "The serpent beguiled me."

Beguiled means deceived. In this case deceived is the same word meaning "creditor or lender." Now man and his church are in debt and are now held accountable both to the image of the serpent as well as by our Father.

Both our Father and the serpent had laid their claim on them. Since they trespassed on another kingdom, they illegally entered another territory without permission. Now they were indebted and had to pay the ruler of that territory.

The fact they ate the food that was not meant for them to eat, meant they were stealing from another kingdom, and now they had to pay the price.

They were lured into a territory and entered a marketplace where they had taken goods that did not belong to them. They were not residents of this evil kingdom, but when they opened the door, they entered in and the Father had to provide an exit or a way out for them. In spite of their sin, He loved them so much that He had to go after them.

Being in another kingdom meant their heavenly authority and power was not operable. He knew they had given up their power and authority to another who now had the power to rule over them.

They were now in a jail cell and the bondage of slavery to another master was now in effect. Now they were held for ransom and were held hostage until the serpent's demands were met.

CHAPTER SEVEN

SATAN'S MOTIVES

Satan clever and cunning, already thought he had won the battle with God in trying to show the other fallen angels that God Himself was a tyrant and now Adam and Eve wanted to be free under his supervision.

Satan stands on a daily basis accusing our Father of His unfairness, by showing how easy it was for others to leave His Holy Kingdom. At the same time, he thought he was so clever that he actually thought that he outsmarted the Father; for now man and the church were now polluted. Therefore if the doctrine is not God's any longer and he has man and the church on his side, they together could overthrow the Kingdom of God. Satan had thought his craftiness and shrewdness produced results that had victory over our Father.

With the fall of man and the church, Satan seen that

Adam and Eve had access to the Tree of Life. Adam and Eve (man and the church) were Satan's key to the Tree of Life. Now he could get to it through them.

If they were to eat of the Tree of Life, sin would contaminate it and consequently sin would live forever. If sin could live forever, then Satan would have the power to overthrow the Throne of the Father. The angelic host would have to serve Satan instead of our Father.

For this reason The Throne of God responded by saying: "Behold, the man has become like one of Us, knowing good and evil; and now, he might stretch out his hand, and take also from the tree of life, and eat, and live forever"— therefore the LORD God sent him out from the garden of Eden, to cultivate the ground from which he was taken. So He drove the man out; and at the east of the garden of Eden He stationed the cherubim and the flaming sword which turned every direction to guard the way to the tree of life.

The verse "man has become like one of Us, knowing good and evil" does not mean that God is both good and evil.

When He spoke the serpent was present. Instead of reading it in the manner of the man has become like God, it should be read as man has become like "one" of Us. The "one" has to do with quantity rather than likeness. One was God and the other was Satan. Therefore Adam and Eve had become like "one" of those who were present.

Man now knew good which was from our Father (Us) and the other was knowing evil which was from the Serpent.

Satan wanted to rule God's Kingdom by ruling over it via pleasure and dictatorship. He wanted to have the authority of Christ and Man. He wanted access to the Tree of Life.

CHAPTER EIGHT

THE TREE OF LIFE

The Tree of Life refers to Christ and the Cross He died upon. Therefore if Satan could gain access to it, he would gain power and authority and a right to rule as he pleased.

In doing so, however, he did not think that God would give His own Son from the Throne to be killed in our place. Therefore, Christ was not only tortured on the Tree of Life, but He also was the Tree of Life, because He became one with it. Therefore when you are truly in Christ, you are One with Him and In Him; where there is no beginning and no end.

Christ had to give His life for man, so that man (we) could be redeemed back to our Father.

The bible says that Christ offered up His life as a sacrifice. This could only mean that Christ offered to be the sacrifice for His Father. He had to go to Our Father and say:

"Please let me be the sacrifice, so that man can be restored and redeemed back to you. I will be the ransom. I'll pay the price because of how much you love them."

So the Father had to agree with the Son and the Spirit of God had to do the Will of the Father. Now the Father Himself had to look at His Son with sadness and compassion. This was His only Son. He wanted more sons and He created man, but man missed the mark and the intentions and focus of what our Father had in mind.

Satan held Adam and Eve as ransom. In order for God to get them back, He would have to pay the ransom price. Jesus offered Himself as that ransom.

Heretofore Christ a humble Son and Servant, was sent upon commission from the Father to restore the inhabitants of His Kingdom. He was to be the sacrifice from His Father to Satan, so that we as man could be purchased back into His Kingdom. This opened a way to abolish the debts incurred from them stealing from another territory.

This was not just any sacrifice. This meant that our Father would have to place His trust in our Brother and in His Son to accomplish what needed to be done. This sacrifice was not just a sacrifice. It was a mission and a dangerous one as well. Why?

It is because sin is a cursed thing. Sin causes separation and a curse is something that "cuts you off "from your inheritance of eternal life. It cuts you off from your Father and from the safety of His protection. It cuts you off from knowing of the mystery in Christ.

Not only did our Father have to trust His Son, but the Son also had to trust His and our Father as well. What united them both was love; the fullness of a Father's love for His Son and a Son's love for His Father.

Jesus would have to fulfill every Word that God spoke out of sheer obedience. He would have to do what He was told to do, and He would have to accomplish it when He was ordered to do so. They both had to have total trust and reliance on one another.

It was also risky. This was sin after all. His only Son was to come into enemy territory and take away what Satan considered to be His.

Thus Satan knew of the plan and he considered what needed to be done, in order for the plan of salvation to be stopped. For now Jesus was on his territory and on his ground.

As long as Jesus did as His Father instructed as He walked through the assignment, He knew His Father would protect Him from eternal death.

We understand now however that Satan did not want Jesus to die on the cross at Calvary.

He tempted Jesus in the wilderness three times, but God was with Him and Satan failed. He tried to tell Him the same lie about death through Peter, when he said "You shall not surely die." However this command of Satan's mouth was not fruitful. Jesus had already known these words, for they were the same words as Satan used on man and the church in the garden. At every turn, Satan and his followers plotted to kill Him. At every opportunity Satan looked to seize Him. At every corner he tried to stop Him from giving that sacrifice; the only sacrifice that would free mankind from his chains of bondage. If he could just get Him to fall, the sacrifice would be blemished. Our Father who is pure and unblemished could not give something that did not belong to Him. Anything blemished would not be of our Father, it would be considered to be from Satan's kingdom. Therefore Jesus life was to be pure and holy as it would be a sacrifice that Satan would not be able to duplicate. This is because the pureness of it was accompanied with the Power of our Father's Will and Spirit.

We see the Father and His Spirit (HIS WILL) descend in order to encourage His Son, so that He could achieve what He was commissioned and sent to do.

At His baptism, the Holy Spirit came and rested upon Him. In the Father's own words He said with admiration: "This is My Son, in Whom I Am Well Pleased."

This was a Word of encouragement and for strengthening, as our Father already knew what Satan was planning.

Jesus spiritually crucified His flesh and went without earthly gratification, in order to strengthen the bond between Him and the Father.

So instead of having Jesus run away Satan, the Holy Spirit led Jesus to him. It was the spirit of God doing the will of God in Jesus that caused Satan's plans to fail. Jesus immersed himself in the water of His word, for He became that Word in the flesh. He was the Word, fulfilling His Father's Word. The Word was to be tested as a witness for others to record. Just as Adam and Eve were tempted, now Jesus was to experience the same.

Satan tried at every instance to derail the Plan of Salvation. He tried every tactic that He could think of, in the hopes of overtaking our Father's Throne.

He tirelessly tempted Jesus to fall, but he could not penetrate that bond between Him and His Father. Satan could not cause Him to sin, for Satan's victory would result in us being permanently separated from our Father.

If Satan could just get Him to separate from His Father, sin would manifest and our Father would be not only shamed but defeated. If Jesus would sin, He would miss the mark or goal that our Father had intended for Him. Jesus offering up Himself would have been a waste of time and would He would lose His heavenly position.

If Jesus would sin He would descend from a higher place to a lower place. He would be thrust down and fall under the judgment of His own Father, thus coming under condemnation. If Jesus would sin, He would descend from an erect and upright position to a low and prostrate position in front of Satan. If this would happen, He would "fallout" or be lost. He would be the cause of being stripped of His Authority and His Power from Our Father.

If Satan could get Him to sin, Jesus would miss out on His inheritance of the saints that Satan was holding captive. If Jesus sinned, He would not be able to have His share in all that is Holy and Pure.

If Jesus would sin, He would come under judgment and would be considered no longer righteous. If Satan could get Him to sin, Jesus would no longer be in right standing with God, and thus lose His heavenly position and would end up giving His heavenly authority over to Satan.

Jesus walked with the bonds of love. He was in chains but only to His Father. He offered Himself up to rescue us, to redeem us, to take us back home. He was sent to pay the ransom.

.

CHAPTER NINE

SIN, LOVE AND HONOR

Being free from sin doesn't mean one is sinless. It doesn't mean you are perfect; rather it is being free from the chains or bondages of sin. It is being free to do what God wishes for one to do, as well as the ability to do accomplish the task given to us.

When one sins, they err or mistake wrong for right. When we sin we wander from the correct path or direction that God has already instilled in us. When Adam and Eve sinned, they placed themselves in a dishonorable position. They dishonored God from the fact they didn't take responsibility.

Lack of responsibility causes us to wonder further and further away from the Truth. T

To honor someone is to give them attention, love and respect in a manner that it is well received. Therefore when we wander, God chases and disciplines us because he loves us, so that we can learn how to bring Him what He requires This in itself is a call to repentance.

Repentance is an opportunity to walk in the goodness of God. It is a door of escape from the bonds of sin. It is an invitation to dine with Him so that we are able to gain His understanding in how much He loves us. Therefore we rejoice through various trials, for we know that it is the growing of our faith in Him that is being tended. He does not want us to be killed or destroyed. Therefore out of His instructions are orders of love, in order that we remain in His protection.

He is The Good Shepherd and lovingly looks after His sheep. Therefore He hedges us in, so that the Word in us will take root and not be swept away by any other doctrine.

His Boundaries

These boundaries of protection are the borders of his outstretched arms. His hands touch each of us as He corrals us into the safety of His Presence.

His protective boundaries; His arms of love are ever present and nothing will ever separate us from that Love. This surety bond of love is ever present, if we choose to have Him lead us, rather than lead ourselves.

All of us are called to be in the fold of Him, but few of us make the choice to honor Him in the manner that He requests.

When we choose to come under the Holy Shepherd's rod, we are choosing to be corrected and taught by whomever He has appointed to do so. We must trust Him with this In order that we can become the chosen people, we are called to be.

When we are "in love" with the understanding of the Father, we submit ourselves to stay within the boundaries of protection and do our best not to wander off to be tempted or lured into other folds that do not honor the Lord God as He is.

Mankind in the beginning wandered away from the path God set forth and the instructions given. Man began to look in another direction and walk away from the borders of safety. When we do the same, we violate God's laws or commands. When understood correctly, these are simply God's instructions and directions.

When we sin, we miss the mark. When we sin we place ourselves in a position to not be able to share in all that God has placed on the other side of His instructions. Therefore it is impossible to fulfill these conditions, if we do not understand the full meaning of sin and repentance.

When we wander from God's instructions (law), we commit an offense, for we have trespassed into a kingdom which is not ours to have.

To trespass is to go beyond the borders from which we are legally entitled. We trespass when we enter another property or jurisdiction that we have not been given permission or authority to enter.

When one wishes to partake of another kingdom and give loyalty of any level to it, they in essence honor it. When one honors it, they give love and respect to it and conform to what that kingdom desires.

Serving another kingdom or deviating from the instruction (law) of God is therefore considered to be high treason against the throne.

This very act separates one from the presence of God, but not from the love of God. God still loves all who depart from Him, but He does not condone rebellious mocking behavior from, those who do not wish to abide in Him.

God loves all people, but He does not love treason or lies against His Holy Presence. We must understand that He is Holy and therefore we are called also to be Holy.

Holiness, love and obedience for Him and his law, bring Him honor and respect. More importantly it depicts our loyalty to Him, so that we may be accounted as His friends, whom serve as 'sons' in His Kingdom. Only sons whom God has joined with him as a kingdom of priests are allowed to serve him upon his throne.

Being a son requires holiness and no evil record must be found in them. There is no room for "high treason" in the judicial courts of the heavens.

What is high treason? High treason is defined as this: criminal disloyalty to one's government. participating in a war against one's native country, attempting to overthrow it's government, spying on its military, it's diplomats, or its secret services for a hostile and foreign power or attempting to kill its head of state are perhaps the best known examples of high treason.

High treason requires that the alleged traitor have obligations of loyalty in the state he or she betrayed, such as citizenship.

When we do not follow the instructions or directions of God, we are committing high treason. This is a "punishable by death" offense. We become a criminal in the courts of heaven and the chains, cufflinks and jail cells become our home and our way of life.

During our incarceration, we are bound in chains and our hands are tied. We are fed what man feeds us and we are caged with no way out. We are separated from the Presence of God, but we are not separated from His love.

He knows we are in our jails, but He wants us to realize where we went wrong; not to condemn us, for we have already been condemned by ourselves and therefore have also shamed ourselves as well as our Father.

Take note that one is only in bonds and chains after the arrest. Man is already condemned through his own actions and not because God was angry and put them there. You cannot see guilt or shame until God arrests you and shows you what you were trying to hide from Him.

Unlike man, God is merciful to forgive, when we make an error in judgment or miss the mark. This forgiveness comes when we choose to walk in His instructions with the determination of our minds and hearts. When our minds and bodies repent and do what is acceptable in His sight, He is pleased and forgives with the love only a Father can give.

Repentance seems to be a foreign thing to a religious mind. It is often accompanied with condemnation either from ourselves as well as from others. These individuals do not understand what sin is and in religious mindsets, one is led to believe they are doomed and must be put through sacrifice in order to get back into "God's good graces."

It is by the love of God, that He brings you to repentance. The fact you feel ashamed or guilty means God has already visited you. Now He only awaits your answer in regards to your responsibility. He wants to know if you can see what you have done. He wants you to see the sin you can acknowledge it. He wants you to identify the wrong and then turn in the right direction, so you can continue to discover Him. He doesn't want you to repeat the Adam and Eve event.

Doing this with pure heart is what being" in" Him is about. This means you are" in" His will and that you will walk, think, live, and breathe on a daily basis accordingly.

Sin is the violation of the commands, law or instructions of God. Though we may not get it perfect, as we continue to walk in pure heart it is then His grace which covers us. That grace is filled with his love, as love covers a multitude of sins.

Note also that there is no condemnation for those who are in Christ Jesus.

If there is no condemnation, then there is no need to condemn others or yourself. Therefore the ones who truly walk in repentance apprehend Whom has apprehended them

CHAPTER TEN

UNDERSTANDING THE BEAST AND 666

The word "understand" also means apprehend or comprehend. Therefore since he chased you and caused you to see your shame, you now have the opportunity to comprehend or understand Him. This joyfully brings you into His Presence and you now have another opportunity to the deeper knowledge of Christ and The Father.

To help you understand further, sin can be symbolically compared to leprosy or a deathly disease, such as spiritual cancer.

The bible states that all have sinned and fall short of the glory of God. Therefore no man can save us from the consequences of sin, except Christ Himself.

As stated previously, sin is a death sentence. It is a "mind disease." It can only be cured by a specialist; an internist that specializes in blood transfusions. One only needs a Physician that can take the curse and its effects away from our lives, and let it reside where it doesn't control our carnal or animalistic spiritual appetites any longer.

This sin is in our genes; our DNA when we are born. Each one of us has it. Sin holds certain structures; certain characteristics that make it sin. It has a mark that has been placed upon it, so that once identified it is judged as whether the carrier will live or die.

Sin is a cursed thing and those who choose to serve it, also come under the same determination.

However, God is so great and so full of love that He gave His only Son to die for what we are accursed to be born into. Christ is the only sacrifice that is necessary to heal cursed DNA. The curse is generational and it has the ability to repeat generation to generation. It is an unclean thing, an evil thing and an impure thing.

Just as DNA has markers for identification, sin also has marks. Therefore anyone within identifier or mark of sin is marked for death. Like land markers that plot out property, so were those who identify with evil doctrine. What the individual believes and what he stands for, these markers determine whether one lives or dies.

Like a plot in a graveyard, their place of non-rest marks out where they serve their god.

God's chosen are also marked out as his property and their deeds are recorded in His book. These deeds include his signature or seal. Those whose names are recorded in the ledger of life are considered his inheritance.

Once the markers have been balanced and identified, each is judged according to whether they will live or whether they will die.

No man has the power to release its power or death sentence. Only Christ has the authority to operate in sending that accursed thing into remission. There is only One that take away the bonds, chains and effects of being a condemned man. There is only One that can send this mindful disease into remission. The greater we distance ourselves from the disease, the more free we become.

What is repentance? It is the turning from sin and dedicating oneself to the amendment of one's life. It is to feel regret for dishonoring God and to change one's mind.

Therefore when we repent, we turn from what we previously thought was correct, and make the turn in the right direction. This 180° turn causes us not to look back but to look ahead. We continue to press on toward the high calling in Christ.

We cannot look ahead however if we focus on our shame and stay believing in pride. We cannot look to Christ in repentance and please others around us who are in opposition. God is holding each of us accountable as individuals. The biggest things that holds one back is ego and pride and the fear that someone might not like the decision we have made.

If we cannot accept that responsibility, we are too prideful to recognize and acknowledge our weaknesses before God.

When we dwell in self-condemnation we deny Christ in the process. If we deny Christ's instruction, we are considered to be stiff-necked because of our refusal to turn.

When we are able to walk in the proper direction it is the evidence that we have received Him. However repentance is not to be taken flippantly or casually or as a thing one takes for granted. Repentance and forgiveness given and received correctly, are the essential key rings that hold the Master's key.

For example, saying that you forgive others, without pure motives is denying Christ. Saying you forgive others and then speak badly them or gossiping about them, is denying Christ. Blessing others using God's name to show superiority or using His name such as" God bless you or have a blessed day", while you are internally cursing them is denying Christ.

Using your gifts for your own grandeur and putting God's name on them is denying Christ. These are just a few examples that require repentance. The morals of the world have dictated the church of our Father for too long. Now all must repent. All must make the turn. All must follow His ways instead of man's ways.

> The church of the world looks like the world. The true church of bride of Christ, bear the marks and the identifiers that separate them from the rest.
>
> Sin operates in the world as a way of life; and now sin operates in the false church as a way of life also.
>
> Whichever doctrine is received is the doctrine that is believed."

What is received is what a person actually does with the doctrine they have ingested whether good or evil. We as a whole have learned many things in regards to sin, and there have been many opinions and suggestions on how to make amends with our Father.

Some churches rationalize sin, others have prayer formulas, others have sacrificial offerings and still others have specific penance they want you to do in order to eradicate the sins you have committed.

There are times when we sin and know it and other times we sin and are unaware of it.

Each one of us has been dealt a life with experiences, people and circumstances. Most of us have learned about

God, through what someone else has told us or learned through the filters they have placed within us.

Many for the most part try to figure God out. They look for the reasons why He does things, rather than on Who He TRULY IS. This only leads to confusion, for they try to learn Him through man's perspective, instead of allowing God to reveal Himself on His own.

This way of thinking only leads to a life of bondage and confusion, for they wish to see Him from the ground up, instead of God's way of wanting us to see things from His perspective. This is why the bible states that our thoughts are not His thoughts and His ways are not our ways.

Therefore walking in Him requires walking "in" righteousness or right standing. To do this we must make the turn. We must turn from sin.

To do this we turn from going backwards to going forwards. We are not to look back at what we previously have done that was incorrect, but we must instead make the 180 degree turn to do what is correct. We are to seek Him and Him alone.

When we physically, mentally, emotionally and spiritually make the turn, we are set and pointed in the right direction.

Repentance turns your face toward God instead of away from Him.

God doesn't condemn an already condemned man. If man makes the turn with His entire being, God accepts it as repentance and you are restored. Our entire mind, body, soul and spirit, turns away from our own personal ideas of what is acceptable and non acceptable in God's eyes. When we make the complete turn, we go into a different direction and the old things no longer are in sight.

. WE reach for what God has and wishes to reveal for us as we grow and walk closer accompanied by His Presence.

We can no longer mix the old life with the new life. This doesn't mean we will not make mistakes, but it does offer us the assurance that God's grace covers us as we walk in the right direction.

Jesus was a lamb just as we are sheep. God the Father gave His Son as a lamb to be slaughtered for the sin of the world; The sin of the whole world, but more importantly the sin of your own personal world.

John the Baptist said "Behold the Lamb of God, who takes away the sin of the world."

What he was actually saying was" **behold the sacrifice of God Himself, the One Who offered and agreed to take away the separation between you and your heavenly Father.**

The Father separated himself to bring us home. All we have to do is repent by the stopping of serving an idea of Him.

Thus when idol worship ceases, your love for Him increases.

Christ was given to the world from our Father. He was given out of God for the purposes of God. He was given to remove the things that would cause us to lose eternal life.

The Father loves his children so much, that He separated Himself, from Himself in order to give us the eternal gift of Life, so that we would no longer have to be separated from "knowing" Him.

The words "takes away the sin of the world" is given in present tense.

When Christ takes away our sins, He removes sin from our foresight (what is in front of us that causes us not to walk in Him). When He removes it or takes it away, He separates the death sentence from us. He then takes the sin and carries it upon Himself. He removes it from our world. The effects of the deathly DNA, no longer need to concern us, as long as we walk in repentance by doing the will and instructions of the Father.

When He removes or takes away the sin, we are given His life and we are saved from the death sentence it incurs. When He removes sin and takes it away, we choose to accept His doctrine in its purity and choose not to put ourselves through self condemnation any longer.

As with any serious illness that causes death, once this disease is placed into remission, we are lifted up and clothed in righteousness or right standing with Him.

With Christ putting our sin into remission, we are daily able to rely on His mercies that are afresh each morning. Each day we are able to distance ourselves at a greater level, the death sentence it carried.

Upon acceptance and submission to His Will, His Spirit teaches us the true identity of our Father. It is one of the benefits; we are given when we receive the spiritual blood transfusion that releases us into His Newness of Life.

As He separates sin from us, we however still hold the DNA responsible for committing violations against God's instructions. Therefore, we must act aggressively not to look back at the former incorrect things and ways that are not of His Kingdom.

If we continue to look back, the temptations of former violations of God's instructions will cause us to be of no seasoning to and for others. The sinful DNA will be touched and a disease that was once in remission, will once again present itself as a death sentence into our lives.

Sin once again is a violation against the instructions of God. It does not matter how many sacrifices you give, how many people you can teach or preach to, how much extra work you do for others or for your church (building or human) or how much money you believe you can give to satisfy God. All of things God calls as reasonable service. We must understand that no dead sacrifice is acceptable to God. We are to present our bodies as living sacrifices that glorify His Temple.

As with any mortal illness that causes death, this sinful leprosy is placed in remission. There it lies dormant. If it is dead in our lives the disease will stay in remission. It no longer has the ability to rule over us, but rather we rule over it instead.

Jesus bore our sicknesses and our infirmities so that we would not be weakened by its effects. **Sin goes into remission as soon as we make the turn.**

Whatever sin needs to be dealt with, God will cause us to look at it so that we can repent of it. This substantiates that his goodness draws us to repentance. **God cannot condemn something He purposely caused you to identify.**

Sin causes you to descend from a higher place to a lower place. When you repent He lifts you up to your former place. He causes you to stand in an upright position.

Each time you repent, you are put in right standing and are declared righteous in His eyes. This does not mean that you have license to sin however.

Additionally we are not authorized to bring ourselves to repentance, for that would put ourselves in Christ's position. Doing this would not be operating in the doctrine of Christ, as we would be operating against him and therefore be considered an antichrist. Whatever is for or according to his doctrine and the perception of how he sees things, is therefore considered pro-Christ or for Christ. Any doctrine or perception not of Christ is against Christ for antichrist.

Our minds, hearts, bodies and souls therefore must listen to the instructions and directions of the Father. We cannot do this without faith, and without faith it is impossible to please Him.

The only thing God wants you to have is eternal life. What is eternal life? Eternal life is "knowing God" and not just "knowing about God."

That is what we are here for and that is the purpose of which you were born.

It's not about how bad or how good you think you are. It's not about what physical or carnal thing you can do for Him; for He is Spirit and Truth and we must worship Him in the same manner.

All that He asks is that you "know Him."

How do you get to know Him?

"Seek Ye First the Kingdom of God and His Righteousness and "All These Things" will be given to you.

Seeking the kingdom of God is seeking the way God does things. It is the searching of His ways. Seeking His Righteousness is seeking what is considered to be right standing in His eyes.

Every one of us is different. Each one of us is like a snowflake, in His eyes; being that no two are the same. Therefore our walks will be different in nature. This means each one of us, must work out our own salvation with fear and trembling. Our walk is between ourselves as individuals and God.

Moreover we are not to judge what another eats or drinks or what day he or she keeps. We are to judge according to our own mirror. If another "seems" to be doing not what we discern is incorrect in the eyes of God or according to how God has taught first hand to us, we are to dust our shoes off and leave. When we understand Christ's mission and relationship with the Father, we understand that God is bringing them to repentance in His own time and through the people He has appointed to work in their lives.

We are not to cast judgments of condemnation, but rather we are to go in peace and pray that others will come to experience the joy of "knowing Him."

The Paradigm Shift

To enable your ability to further understand repentance or the paradigm shift, I will tell you a journey of a person who went to the doctor because of a blood pressure problem.

In the doctor's office, this person was told that they could not live if they continued to live in the manner they were living much longer. They were told that if they didn't have a paradigm shift in their thinking they would have to be placed on medication for the rest of their life.

So the doctor told the person if they didn't turn from what they had been doing , for example what they were doing and what they were eating, they would certainly live a life tied and bound to heart disease and medication. They had to make a paradigm shift. This person had to make a turn. They had already been given a diagnoses and a death sentence was pronounced.

This person didn't need someone else to worsen the situation by adding on to the seriousness of it. This person didn't need "I told you so" over and over again. This person didn't need even more stress placed upon them. No amount of money or sacrifice could eradicate the situation. The only thing that was to be done that would produce wellness and life, was a turn in their mind and heart that would produce a different behavior.

The person went home and made a change; a turn in their way of thinking and was evident in their doing. They began to see food and exercise differently and could see the results immediately.

Each day the weight came off of them. Each day the effects of the burden of heaviness, became more evident, as they became lighter and lighter.

What they did and what they ate produced a new way of life. What they needed was already there, but no one was there to educate and point them in the right direction.

The further into the newness of life, the greater the manifestation of their decision. As the weight dropped, their clothes changed. Their outlook was different. They had someone to tell them the right way and to lead them in the right direction.

Once the person acknowledged the lifestyle they were living was not good for life, they changed it. Then they started to walk in a different direction. The person stayed away from the things that could kill them and replaced them with the things that would give them life.

Though this is just a fictional story, it should help you with a picture of what repentance looks like.

What God is Concerned About

What really is the sin that God is concerned about? Is it all the bad things we do or the lack of doing what we think we should do? Sin in God's eyes is transgression of the law.

Since Christ died on the cross for the purposes of redemption, we must make the decision to give over to

Him that which He died for. In a sense they are His, for He has taken ownership of them.

Taking back what He took away from us, is therefore like taking someone else's property. In this case Christ took what we were not to touch in the first place and placed it upon Himself.

He holds the titles on the property deeds of the dust, as the Bible states we are made from the dust.

Satan is given dust to eat and he can only eat what agrees with him. Therefore so that you do not trespass or transgress the laws or the commands meant for man, they themselves stand as signposts which say" wrong way!"

The 10 Commandments are the laws or instructions of God for man. If one does not stay within the boundaries of the law, one comes under the law. This means the law now rules over you rather than through you.

Let me explain. If a person steals a loaf of bread from a store, he is now subject to the ruling authorities. The law (police, judge etc) places him in bondage through handcuffs, jail cells etc. This person is now under the law, meaning that the law rules over him. He is subject to whatever they say and he has no freedom.

If a person keeps within the boundaries of the law, meaning he does what is required in the law, God lives through them. This means they have freedom in it, rather than the torment of being under it.

Thus, those who live by the sword, die by the sword. The sword is the Word of Truth. We choose whether to live by it or die by it.

The Truth is God's instruction and is accompanied by God's direction. We are His land, for we are made from the earth; from the dust of the earth. Therefore we are His property. He holds the deed to our land. He therefore is our "Landlord."

Each one of us is a kingdom that is to serve unto Him. We are called to be a kingdom of priests that serve our God; not a king and a priest.

Being that we are so ingratiated with His goodness from the very fact we are placed here, is a testament that He is a living God. He rules over His land continually and what we choose to form ourselves into is of our own free will. We are a fruitful land and because we are so valuable we must be watchful that we do not enter into another's kingdom or their ways.

That means it's considered trespassing when one enters into someone else's territory, without authorization. Trespassing is also known as a transgression. Another word for transgression is regression.

Regression is the process that causes one to go back or to regress. In spiritual terms it is sin that causes us to regress or go back to what we were instructed not to enter into.

What was in remission has now been touched and therefore what one touches, has the tendency to cause us to regress back into what

The Marks of the Man of Sin

A worthless person, a wicked man,
Walks with a perverse mouth;
[13] He winks with his eyes,
He shuffles his feet,
He points with his fingers;
[14] Perversity *is* in his heart,
He devises evil continually,
He sows discord.
[15] Therefore his calamity shall come suddenly;
Suddenly he shall be broken without remedy.

Identifying the Abomination that Causes Desolation

These six *things* the LORD hates,
Yes, seven *are* an abomination to Him:
[17] A proud look,
A lying tongue,
Hands that shed innocent blood,

[18] A heart that devises wicked plans,
Feet that are swift in running to evil,
[19] A false witness *who* speaks lies,
And one who sows discord among brethren.

We accept human testimony, but God's testimony is greater because it is the testimony of God, which he has given about his Son. Whoever believes in the Son of God accepts this testimony. Whoever does not believe God has made him out to be a liar, because they have not believed the testimony God has given about his Son. [11] And this is the testimony: God has given us eternal life, and this life is in his Son. [12] Whoever has the Son has life; whoever does not have the Son of God does not have life.

Satan's Name and The Value of His Doctrine

Worthless

The Bible defines the word worthless as: disqualified; failed the test; rejected; reprobate; useless idols

Titus Chapter 1 verse 16:

They profess to know God but their deeds they deny him, being detestable and disobedient and worthless for any good deed.

Romans Chapter 1 verse 28

And just as they did not see fit to acknowledge God any longer, God gave them over to add depraved mind, to do those things which are not proper.

Second Corinthians Chapter 13 verse five

Test yourselves to see if you are in the faith; examine yourselves. Or do you not recognize this about yourselves that Jesus Christ is in you – unless indeed you failed the test?

Satan's name is worthless. The number of his name is worthless. The image he presents is worthless. Satan is described as good for nothing. Those who speak out for him speak curses and blessings out of their vain mouths. They are devoid of the Truth. They operate on plans and schemes of how to get miracles from God, therefore their actions and requests are fruitless.

The word "worthless" in Greek is spelled Poneros and is used in the nominative case in regards to Satan this is the word for Satan's title Jesus refers to him as" the evil one."

The man who follows him is one who is reduced to begging offer asking for alms or offerings. They are destitute of the wealth of wisdom of the father and they are destitute of the Christian virtues and eternal riches. The root word from this word of worthless Strong's number 4098 and the word is "Pipto." Pipto means to "descend from a higher place to a lower place." It means to fall under judgment and to come under condemnation; To lose authority and to come to an end. It also means to be thrust down, to fail in participating in, and to miss a share or partaker in.

(This is what Satan tried to have Jesus do in the wilderness. He wanted Him to cast Himself down.)

Revelation 13 states verses 18

And he causeth all, both small and great, rich and poor, free and bond, to receive a mark in their right hand, or in their foreheads:

[17] And that no man might buy or sell, save he that had the mark, or the name of the beast, or the number of his name.

[18] Here is wisdom. Let him that hath understanding count the number of the beast:

for it is the number of a man; and his number is Six hundred threescore and six.

Now that you have gained wisdom, you shall receive understanding as to the number, the name and the and the number of his name.

Here is wisdom:

Here is the wisdom that belongs to man. Here is the intelligence required to determine events and discovering the meaning of some of this mysterious number. Here is the brand of wisdom that comes from man, who are not disciples of Christ, who use skill and discretion in imparting" Christian" truth.

Here are those who are philosophers and or Raiders, those who are theologians and Christian teachers, who from their best plans, execute their best thoughts and develop their own brand of wisdom.

But this wisdom does not give you automatic understanding. So let him, the individual, who has understanding relayed the message. The individual, the inner man, who is joined in bonds of marriage with what they have possessed and taken hold of the truth; comprehend the powers of good and evil. Recognize what is good and what is evil. Judge soberly. Judge calmly and spiritually. Look at your thoughts, your feelings, your purposes and desires. Get to know the knowledge in the Father, so that you can perceive, comprehend and apprehend all that is Christ and He will be able to compute, as well as understand how many or the number of the lower evil nature of man.

Now this concerns the "number" that have not repented. Comprehend how many are in the multitude that comprise of this tribe. Perceive with your mind those of the lower nature, the carnal man and those who eat dust as the serpent eats. For that indefinite number is a tribe, and that tribe is in man and that man is in the tribe. The man that identifies with this tribe is a merchant man. He buys and is indebted to whom he has stolen from. This man cannot and does not have the ability to pay the price. This man is an individual in the multitude and the multitude is in him. These individuals follow after their own kind. They are a mixed race. They are tribe.

Their number as stated in the King James version is:

600 threescore and six.

600 threescore is 600 times the value of 20.

The prophetic value of 600 is "full reward or wages due."

A threescore has the value of 20,

The value of twenty is symbolic for redemption.

Therefore 600 threescore is equal to 600x20.

This is equivalent to 12,000.

12,000 is equivalent to one tribe.

12 represents order.

1000 represents maturity or full status

The great city as described in Revelation 21:16 is 12,000 stadia.

Stadia is a term that checks weights and balances.

The verse says 600 threescore and six.

The word **AND** is translated as KAI in the Greek, which means" indeed or even or likewise.

Therefore the verse translated by reckoning the values of this verse as follows:

This tribe of man is of its own wisdom. But there to the one who understands in the Father's perception is this: This tribe is indeed a tribe of mankind, whom has given birth to his own kind but does not have the ability to deliver himself.

Whatever image this portrays itself to be is not Me, and therefore they worship a beast. The same beast in the garden. This idea is engrained into their minds. This image is a concept of Whom I Am made out to be.

Therefore whoever receives (doctrine) this concept of Me, or whomever does or partakes of what this (doctrine) gives out what this (doctrine) will carry its precepts.

A mark is an something that is engraved or engrained or etched into someone's mind. It is an image formed in the imagination in other words. It is an idea that produces an image without the need to seek God. It is an image that individuals have given life to that is completely worthless. This image stands where Christ's holiness should stand. This image or idea was formed from the combination of mixed, polluted doctrine. This image has two heads. One head is of Christ and the other is of the evil one. It is the image similar to a coin. (One coin with two sides).

The image of "the evil one" is an idea that is an abomination to our Father. This is an abomination that causes things to be desolate. It is worthless and does not have life until someone refuses to repent.

A persons refusal to repent gives life to this image and causes" the evil one" to stand in the holy place and therefore he or she, gives their full permission for the evil one to lead their lives. The holy place is the place reserved for Christ alone.

And he causeth all, both small and great, rich and poor, free and bond, to receive a mark in their right hand, or in their foreheads:

The verse states that he causes ALL to receive a mark in their right hand or forehead.

Anything placed in the right hand is marked as a sign of vow or allegiance. One raises their right hand to testify to the fact that what they are saying is the Truth.

Isaiah 44

[20] Such a person feeds on dust (ashes);a deluded heart misleads him;
he cannot save himself, or say,
"Is not this thing in my right hand a lie."

Psalms 144:8

Whose mouths speak deceit,

And whose right hand is a right hand of falsehood.

The verse also states "or" forehead. If what the person has determined Him to be in their mind will give one an idea or concept of Him that can also be determined to be a lie. Therefore when we are born in the natural, we are born with the ideas and concepts of those before us. However, God alone knows His children in only the manner that He has created them. So consequently when we are born, mankind's fall caused us to receive a doctrine which distorts the image of our Father.

There is one lie in the bible that perpetuates all others. In order to deal with the others you must deal with the root of matter. Therefore the one lie that caused all others began in the garden with Christ. A lie in God's eyes is no different from anything else. When one sins they are lying to God and themselves. They say they love Him by following another god that has no power and doesn't exist. Therefore if you are always dealing with evil things, the evil one is the one you serve.

[11] And for this reason God will send them strong delusion, that they should believe **the lie**,[12] that they all may be condemned who did not believe the truth but had pleasure in unrighteousness.

Until we have repented and seek God out of love for Him, we will remain in the same state.

[17] And that no man might buy or sell, save he that had the mark, or the name of the beast, or the number of his name.

The individuals in this tribe cannot buy or sell their redemption, for there is no power in the gods they have made themselves appear to be. They do not have the currency of the Kingdom which is the Blood of Christ. He has not redeemed them.

They are indebted to the same serpent as in the garden. They have taken what does not belong to them and therefore they cannot buy themselves with their own blood, neither can they sell themselves with their own blood. The only blood with any value that is worth the price of redemption is Christ's blood through the Power of Repentance.

The image of what they believe is the Truth is not the Truth. Therefore their version is a lie.

A lie is something that is false; it's a vain imagination, a false pretense and is not real.

[18] Here is wisdom. Let him that hath understanding count the number of the beast:

for it is the number of a man; and his number is Six hundred threescore and six.

Therefore the number 666 represents mankind's acceptance of wickedness, evil, mixed or false doctrine, man's pride and arrogance and weakness of humanity in the flesh. It represents man's ideas and the non acceptance of God's Truth. Six is the number of man, for God made man in six days. So man (6) has added, denied and rejected the 66 books as God has given through and to mankind. They therefore have developed and worked through their own interpretation instead of God's interpretation of His scriptures (Word). There are three 6's. These three sixes also represent the denying of the Father, The Son and The Holy Spirit. Each is an attack against the Authority, The Redemption and the Power of God. Peter denies Christ three times in the wilderness. Peter denied Christ three times before the crucifixion. Man's ideas of what heavenly authority, redemption and the power of God is very misleading since it is based on man's interpretation of His 66 books.

Man Within the Image

Daniel 3

3 Nebuchadnezzar the king made an image of gold, whose height *was* sixty cubits *and* its width six cubits. He set it up in the plain of Dura, in the province of Babylon.

This is the example that God allowed for man to see what they were and are still doing. Man formed an image with gold. Gold is the most valuable form of currency in the world. The image was made of what they believed to be the most valuable in order to give honor to the one they believed was God. They believed that the "IMAGE or CONCEPT" they had drawn up was God.

The measurements represent man's ability to save them within the power of this image. However if we were to read the entire story, we see that the only One that saved Shadrach, Meshach and Abednego was Christ, who was in the fire with them. They were saved because they didn't bow down to a concept, but went into death, honoring the Truth.

God's Accounting Methods

The Ledger of All Accounts

Revelation 18 verses 15

[11] Then I saw a great white throne and him who was seated on it. The earth and the heavens fled from his presence, and there was no place for them. [12] And I saw the dead, great and small, standing before the throne, and books were opened. Another book was opened, which is the Book of Life. The dead were judged according to what they had done as recorded in the books. [13] The sea gave up the dead that were in it, and death and Hades gave up the dead that were in them, and each person was judged according to what they had done. [14] Then death and Hades were thrown into the lake of fire. The lake of fire is the second death. [15] Anyone whose name was not found written in the Book of Life was thrown into the lake of fire.

Double Entry Accounting

Double entry accounting means that for every entry (or entries) made to the debit side of accounts, equal entry (entries) must be made to the credit side of the accounts.

ILLUSTRATION OF A "T" ACCOUNT

ACCOUNT NAME AND NUMBER

(DEBIT)	CREDIT
DR...	CR

With the use of various levels of technology in governmental accounting, the "T" account no longer is visible in computer systems. However, an awareness of the concept of the "T" account is useful in understanding double entry accounting.

The books in heaven are somewhat like accounting books and each time we repent of the things that God hates, it is credited to our account.

When we repent and walk in the faith of God, just as Abraham, this is credited to our account of righteousness.

Romans 4

What then shall we say that Abraham, our forefather according to the flesh, discovered in this matter? [2] If, in fact, Abraham was justified by works, he had something to boast about—but not before God. [3] What does Scripture say? "Abraham believed God, and it was credited to him as righteousness." [4] Now to the one who works, wages are not credited as a gift but as an obligation. [5] However, to the one who does not work but trusts God who justifies the ungodly, their faith is credited as righteousness. [6] David says the same thing when he speaks of the blessedness of the one to whom God credits righteousness apart from works:

[7] "Blessed are those
   whose transgressions are forgiven,
   whose sins are covered.
[8] Blessed is the one
   whose sin the Lord will never count against them."
[9] Is this blessedness only for the circumcised, or also for the uncircumcised? We have been saying that Abraham's faith was credited to him as righteousness. [10] Under what circumstances was it credited? Was it after he was circumcised, or before? It was not after, but before!
[11] And he received circumcision as a sign, a seal of the righteousness that he had by faith while he was still uncircumcised. So then, He is the father of all who believe but have not been circumcised, in order that righteousness might be credited to them.

God Holds Each One of Us as Individuals As Accountable- The Accounting Books of Heaven

The following is an picture of how God determines repentance, so that you can be recorded in the Book of

Life. What you will see is term of accounting called "double entry accounting."

It keeps record of debits and credits. It is the official record of where God is accountable to Himself and bears witness to the judicial courts in heaven. It pertains to all how will be judged.

Revelation 20:12

Then I saw a great white throne and Him who sat upon it, from whose presence earth and heaven fled away, and no place was found for them. And I saw the dead, the great and the small, standing before the throne, and books were opened; and another book was opened, which is *the book* of life; and the dead were judged from the things which were written in the books, according to their deeds. And the sea gave up the dead which were in it, and death and Hades gave up the dead which were in them; and they were judged, every one *of them* according to their deeds. Then death and Hades were thrown into the lake of fire. This is the second death, the lake of fire. And if anyone's name was not found written in the book of life, he was thrown into the lake of fire.

Ex 32:30–35

Now it came to pass on the next day that Moses said to the people, "You have committed a great sin. So now I will go up to the LORD; perhaps I can make atonement for your sin." [31] Then Moses returned to the LORD and said, "Oh, these people have committed a great sin, and have made for themselves a god of gold! [32] Yet now, if You will forgive their sin—but if not, I pray, blot me out of Your Book which You have written."

³³ And the LORD said to Moses, "Whoever has sinned against Me, I will blot him out of My book. ³⁴ Now therefore, go, lead the people to *the place* of which I have spoken to you. Behold, My Angel shall go before you. Nevertheless, in the day when I visit for punishment, I will visit punishment upon them for their sin."

³⁵ So the LORD plagued the people because of what they did with the calf which Aaron made. [1]

Account of the Evil One

The Unrepentant Man

ILLUSTRATION OF A "T" ACCOUNT

ACCOUNT NAME AND NUMBER

(DEBIT)	CREDIT
DR...	CR

Account Name Worthless-

The number of the multitude-Non Exact-The Number of a man; any man; his number is 6 meaning man; the inner man, the rebellious man; the man of sin

Debits	Credits
What are worthless and (DR)............	No Repent
wicked people like?	
They are constant liars (DR),	No Repent
[13] signaling their deceit	
with a wink of the eye, (DR)	No Repent
a nudge of the foot,	
or the wiggle of fingers.(DR)	No Repent
[14] Their perverted hearts	
plot evil,	
and they constantly	
stir up trouble.(DR)	No Repent
[15] But they will be destroyed	
suddenly, broken in an instant	
beyond all hope of healing.	
[16] There are six things	
The LORD hates—	
no, seven things he detests:	
[17] haughty eyes (DR),...............	No Repent
a lying tongue, (DR)	No Repent
hands that kill the	

innocent,(DR)   No Repent
¹⁸ a heart that plots evil,
   feet that race to   (DR)   No Repent
do wrong,
¹⁹ a false witness (DR)   No Repent
who pours out lies,
   a person who sows (DR)   No Repent
discord in a family.

Checks and Balances
Debt is still owed.   The wages of sin is death.

Account of the Righteous Man

The Repentant Man

ILLUSTRATION OF A "T" ACCOUNT

ACCOUNT NAME AND NUMBER

(DEBIT)	CREDIT
DR...	CR

Account Name An Heir

–Priest-son of God

Debits	Credits
What are worthless and .... wicked people like?
They are constant liars, [13] signaling their deceit	Repented (CR)

with a wink of the eye,	Repented (CR)
a nudge of the foot,	
or the wiggle of fingers.	Repented (CR)
⁴ Their perverted hearts	
plot evil, and they constantly	
stir up trouble.	Repented (CR)

¹⁵ But they will bed estroyed suddenly,
   broken in an instant beyond all hope of healing.

¹⁶ There are six things	
the LORD hates—	
no, seven things he detests:	
¹⁷ haughty eyes,…………………….	Repented (CR)
a lying tongue,	Repented(CR)
hands that kill the	
innocent,	Repented (CR)
¹⁸ a heart that plots evil,	
feet that race to	Repented (CR)
do wrong,	
¹⁹ a false witness	Repented (CR)
who pours out lies,	
a person who sows	Repented(CR)
discord in a family.	

Checks and Balances

The Wages of His Works is Life   Debt is Paid in Full.
Righteousness has been credited to this account.
He is forgiven of all his debts, which he inherited from his mankind.
This name is now written in the Book of Life.

Christ is the visual crowning glory of redemption. All debts are paid by Him and through Him. There is no other means of redemption. The crucifixion demonstrates not only His overcoming sin, but He points us to look at what the Cross holds, so that we will understand the parameters of our Father's love and forgiveness.

Crowning Conclusion

The crown of thorns represents how we too can overcome sin by looking at what the power of repentance and redemption can do.

Jesus fulfilled the Father's Word and manifested the fruit of that Word in real time. The thorns on His Head were a depiction of how He is able to overcome sin completely.

Thorns choke out plants or trees as they grow. A crown of thorns was placed on His head, because Christ became the embodiment of sin. The Crown of Thorns represented His Royalty and His Authority to overcome or choke out anything that comes under His Power and Authority.

Therefore the thorns on Christ's head choked out the body of sin.

Mathew 13.

[7] Other seeds fell among thorns, and the thorns grew up and choked them out.

The crown of thorns was placed and twisted on His head, because He claimed to be King of the Jews.

This represents the false claims and the twisted doctrine. This claim that He was King of the Jews was not correct, as He was also the King of the Gentiles (non Jews), for they were grafted in on the Cross. In other words their sins were grafted or cut into Christ, the Tree of Life.

The head represents anything supreme. Therefore, the crown on His head relates to the extreme or supreme punishment and loss of Life.

Symbolically the crown cuts off the head of sin. It strangles sin from breathing or causing it to give life on its own strength.

His entire body was beneath the Crown. Therefore whatever is beneath the crown, is under the commands and Authority of The Throne. Everything had to come into submission under the crown, for now the only One who could not choke out life of sin, was the Father Himself.

As The Father looked down on His Son, He saw the sins of the world. He saw all the rebellion and hate of the evil one, and after being clothed in glory, He was now clothed in sin.

The glory from His Father was no longer seen, and He was naked before the world and His Father. Just as mankind in the garden, both man and Christ were now naked before God. It was sinful and there was a moment of suspension as He was hanging on the cross.

Both arms were stretched out, as He offered Himself up to pay our ransom. On both arms hang all the law that He upheld. His body upheld the commands and instructions of His Father.

He stood naked physically and spiritually, before His Father and now there was a separation. This separation was caused by sin itself.

Now Jesus had to trust His Father to forgive the sins of world. In other words now Jesus had to trust His Father to forgive Him. Now the Father had to show the world the love involved when one repents. Christ and His holiness became both the human embodiment of sin. This was the physical manifestation of mixed doctrine of good and evil.

Our Father actually had to forgive His own Son, because He became the sins of the world; and now His Father also had to **remember** what He had done for Him and mankind.

Malachi 3:16

[16] Then they that feared the LORD spake often one to another: and the LORD hearkened, and heard it, and a book of remembrance was written before him for them that feared the LORD, and that thought upon his name.

When Christ was on the cross, He cried out, "My God , Abba, Father! Why hast thou forsaken me?" or Papa why have you left Me? Why have you forgotten about Me?

Why have you deserted Me? Why have you turned your back on Me? Why have you left Me? Where did you go? I sacrificed My life for You! Where did you go? I did what you asked Me to do! Why did you abandon Me? Why did you separate from Me? Why did you cut me off? Why did you cease to be with Me? Where are you? I cannot see you! I cannot hear you! Father please don't leave Me, I don't want to die without You!

For one moment in time, our Father paused for a moment, as His only Son was caused to fall from an erect, higher and right standing position to a lower and prostrate position.

Now the Father had to look at every mark of disobedience we have or could ever do. Now not only did He have to look at His only Son and feel the shame and pain of sin upon Him, but He also had to forgive.

Now the responsibility of sin was placed in the our Father's hands and now was the moment of Truth!

There was silence in heaven. The Father and Jesus, both broken hearted The silence was unbearable as Jesus cried out because of the separation.

Would the Father stand and uphold His Word; would He forgive His Son, so that we could be free from the grips and bonds of sin. These chains were what bound us or forced us to live in exile. Until ransom is paid, hostages could not be freed. For now we are free to worship Him in the manner He desires. We are free to do as we are called to do, if we choose. Jesus paid the ransom note. The note was His life.

The value of man's life verses the only Son of God is somewhat mind boggling. God offers up purity in His sacrifice, while the evil one offers up dead things that cannot walk, talk or breathe. The only way they have life is if mankind breathes life into them and gives them a breath to survive.

Thus those who worship evil doctrine give God's breath to them in order to give it life. He calls it an abomination. God allows free will so that we will come to worship Him out of love, instead of necessity or wrong motives. This in itself should show us how much our Father loves us.

To understand Jesus sacrifice, one must know the hidden mystery that happened between Him and Our Father. Jesus the only begotten Son of God, was His Word.

The crucifixion was the event where our Father had to look at not only His Son but also His Word. There they were with both of them were being sacrificed and held up for scourging and death.

When Jesus cried out "Forgive them they know not what they do," he was telling His Father that they do not understand who You are. Therefore when He died misunderstanding died with Him also. For all are to go to Him that are burdened down with religion instead of being unburdened when walking in Repentance.

If Jesus died and the Father did not forgive, then the Word would also die. If the Word died without resurrection, the evil one, would win the war in the heavens and ultimately have authority over all mankind.

The two doctrines were evident throughout the crucifixion event. There were two thieves on the Cross. One took responsibility and the other didn't. In other words he wanted Jesus to sin before He was to take on the sacrifice. If Jesus would have done this, the sacrifice would have been made null and void.

Not only that but Jesus as well as the rest of us would have ended up serving Satan as his slaves and servants and giving him our honor by obeying and carrying out his version of the lie of mixed doctrine.

Out of the Tree of Knowledge of Good and evil came the spiritual paper that people have believed and trusted in. Jesus fulfilled being the Tree of Life. It is the tree where the spiritual paper of Truth comes from.

The knowledge of good and evil without repentance causes you to be double minded and hypocritical. It leaves you bound and wandering to places where angels dare not tread.

Adam and Eve did not take responsibility, but Christ did. The same forgiveness was available to Adam and Eve if they would have wanted it, but they didn't. If they would have repented they would have taken responsibility for their decisions and consequent actions.

Therefore the same forgiveness He gave His Son, is the same forgiveness, He gives us if we make the turn and repent.

It's the same forgiveness we will have if we take responsibility and acknowledge and cry out to our Father.

Repenting is not just saying I'm sorry. It is not just a word. Jesus died so that you would know that if His Father could forgive Him, He can also forgive you. When we turn towards God, we are not cut off, for it is at the moment of turning we are already restored. It is then we are able to walk in according to His instructions.

Jesus died so that you can be saved through repentance. The sinners prayer is not repentance. It takes no conviction to recite some words. It requires no commitment to change to repeat what someone has told you to do. To accept Jesus as your Savior, you must understand what He did to save you from the death sentence it incurs. It is a new covenant established so that you may live IN Him. To live In Him simply means to live within the means of God. When someone is trying to learn how to budget their life, they have to learn how to live within their means. When it comes to salvation, one has to learn how to live within the means or the boundaries that Christ has set forth. However it is not automatic if you are not repentant.

The cross is a cross of salvation, so that we know how to live in a repentant state. This is how you overcome by the

Blood of the Lamb. In order to repent, you must know that He is and that He is a rewarder for those who seek Him.

" For it is the goodness of God that leads you to repentance."

Repentance causes you to walk towards Him so that you can seek Him.

The cross is the manifestation of repentance and its rewards.

If you want the veil of your temple to be rent in two so that you can see clearly; Repent!

If you want Christ to raise you in the same company as all His saints; Repent!

If you want God to shake the earth to bring all to repentance; Repent!
If you want the power of the Holy Spirit in you, so you can walk with others as they repent; Repent!

If you believe in the sacrifice of the Lord God and the price He had to pay for your ransom; Repent!

If you believe and are willing to accept His Truth and exhibit the willingness to be taught; Repent.

If you are willing to have your present faith tested to see if it is Truth; Repent!

If you are willing to trust the Lord even unto death, with

all your heart and all your soul and all your being; Repent!

Repentance brings the resurrection. Don't die broken hearted and left for dead, because of the lie that has been placed in you.

Turn and walk in the newness of Christ and you shall be made whole

Acts 2:38

[38] Peter answered them, "All of you must turn to God and change the way you think and act, and each of you must be baptized in the name of Jesus Christ so that your sins will be forgiven. Then you will receive the Holy Spirit as a gift. [39] This promise belongs to you and to your children and to everyone who is far away. It belongs to everyone who worships the Lord our God."

John 3:16

[16] God loved the world this way: He gave his only Son so that everyone who believes in him will not die but will have eternal life

The Ten Commandments

Exodus 20 And God spoke all these words:

> **2** "I am the LORD your God, who brought you out of Egypt, out of the land of slavery.

3 "You shall have no other gods before me.

4 "You shall not make for yourself an image in the form of anything in heaven above or on the earth beneath or in the waters below. 5 You shall not bow down to them or worship them; for I, the LORD your God, am a jealous God, punishing the children for the sin of the parents to the third and fourth generation of those who hate me, 6 but showing love to a Thousand generations of those who love me and keep my commandments.

7 "You shall not misuse the name of the LORD your God, for the LORD will not hold anyone guiltless who misuses his name.

8 "Remember the Sabbath day by keeping it holy. 9 Six days you shall labor and do all your work, 10 but the seventh day is a Sabbath to the LORD your God. On it you shall not do any work, neither you, nor your son or daughter- nor your male or female servant, nor your animals, nor any foreigner residing in your towns. 11 For in six days the LORD

made the heavens and the earth, the sea, and all that is in them, but he rested on the seventh day. Therefore the LORD blessed the Sabbath day and made it holy. **12** "Honor your father and your mother, so that you may live long in the land the LORD your God is giving you.

13 "You shall not murder.

14 "You shall not commit adultery.

15 "You shall not steal.

16 "You shall not give false testimony against your neighbor. **17** "You shall not covet your neighbor's house. You shall not covet your neighbor's wife, or his male or female servant, his ox or donkey, or anything that belongs to your neighbor."

Our Father created the church and the church was taken out of man's side; thus the church was born. Upon Jesus dying on the cross, a soldier pierced Jesus side and blood and water came out, and the New Church was birthed. The Lord promised that rivers of living water will flow out of us if we believe and walk in His Will

Repent and the
mark of the beast
shall be taken from you.
Remove the Anti-Christ,
The man of rebellion in you.

FOR ADDITIONAL COPIES OF THIS BOOK FOR YOUR CHURCH OR BIBLE STUDY GROUP VISIT US ONLINE AT

WWW.THEOCRACYHOUSE.COM

BULK PURCHASING OF BOOKS

EMAIL INFO@KINGDOMGOV.COM

VISIT US ON FACEBOOK
WWW.FACEBOOK.COM/KINGDOMGOV

SPEAKING OR TEACHING INQUIRIES
MEDIA@SOPHIACALLOWAY.COM

www.ingramcontent.com/pod-product-compliance
Lightning Source LLC
Chambersburg PA
CBHW050652160426
43194CB00010B/1909